Gardening For kids

Learn Gardening basics, Grow, Harvest, and Enjoy your Gardening

By Daphne M Cooper

This book belongs to

_____

Table of Contents

Just for You

A free gift to our readers

http://daphnemcooper.com/parenting.pdf

Joining the PME Community

Looking to meet other parents that can help you on your parenting journey? If so, then check out the Parenting Made Easy (PME) Community here:

https://www.facebook.com/groups/293830159257919/

Introduction

Have you ever wondered how food gets from the farm to your plate? Have you ever seen a baby plant grow into a big fat strawberry? Kids who garden get to watch their food grow from seeds into something delicious. They explore the smells and colors of flowers, trees, and vegetables.

They get to touch them!

It's a chance to walk barefoot, dig in the dirt, and play with worms. A great way to keep active and stay healthy too. I wrote this book to give you a chance to experience this feeling for yourself. I am sure every day someone tells you not to watch TV or not to play your video games so much. But often nobody tells you what else you can do.

Well, I am here to change that. Today I am going to tell you about an enjoyable and rewarding activity that you can do.

You guessed it right; I am talking about gardening!

So, What is gardening?

Gardening is the process of growing plants for your own benefit or enjoyment. It can be anything from a tiny herb garden in your patio to massive fields used to produce crops. You might think it's an adults-only hobby. But it is not only for them. Everyone can do gardening, young or old, and you don't need any experience to start either!

You may need adult supervision, but I am sure by the end of reading this book, you're going to surprise everyone with your skills and knowledge.

My experience with gardening.

My love for gardening started from an early age. Over time, I experienced that gardening can be a lot of fun and an excellent way to spend your time. It is excellent for the environment because you improve your surroundings, and it helps out local wildlife too.

Watching leaves grow into bigger plants was a part of my joy as a kid and I always kept my love for gardening alive. So, when I became a mother, I found the perfect way to pass it on. After all, what can be more fun than playing in the mud and learning about the magic of nature!

Once you get fresh, healthy food that you picked yourself, you won't be able to resist it. My kids also experienced that joy, and now they are my partners in our garden.

That's why I wrote this book, to give you a secret gateway for having a common hobby with adults around you.

What to expect from this book?

From the fundamental knowledge about gardening basics to planting gardens and harvesting, you will learn it all very fast! Of course, I am not just talking about fun facts here; I am also including all the practical bits you need to know before buying tools and planting seeds.

Even if you don't like the outside or have no outside space, you can always start a small garden on your balcony or on your windowsill. Whatever fits your needs, I will give you all the tips and tricks.

But before that, you might want to know, why is gardening a good hobby for you?

Gardening is a fun activity that allows you to get in touch with nature and enjoy the greenery. It also teaches you responsibility since you will have to water your plants every day and make sure all the pests are gone before harvesting. It can be a great way of gaining experience in working with tools, and your family will enjoy it too.

But most importantly, gardening is a fun activity that can turn you into a proud gardener who always has fresh vegetables to share with friends and family. The only thing you need to do is start!

You can do it by yourself or with friends to have fun while learning something new. The greatest part is that everyone will be pleased with what you're doing since you're assisting Mother Nature!

This is one of the most important reasons gardening is popular among humans since it benefits the environment.

Impacts of Gardening

Gardening is a great activity for the planet since it involves producing food while using sustainable ways. So basically, you're growing your own little ecosystem in a pot.

What's more, your garden will attract all sorts of wildlife that can help with pest control and pollination. Expect a lot of butterflies and birds around your homegrown flowers and plants. While gardening is a great hobby on its own, it improves the overall conditions for life around you!

And last but not least, gardening is a great way to increase self-esteem and help with stress relief. After all, you can't be stressed if you're busy taking care of your garden every day.

As you spend more and more time in your garden, you will get better at it.

You will know what to do and when to do it because you are the one who has full control over this small ecosystem. It may sound funny that something so simple can have such a deep impact on your mood but hear me out.

It might start as leisure, but soon enough, it will turn into a way of life for you. Once you start taking care of your own little garden, you will be in full control of all the factors affecting it.

Of course, you can't control the weather so much, but you'll learn what plants grow better in which conditions and why.

You also won't have to worry about your plants getting eaten up by bugs; instead, you will get used to checking for pests and treating them all yourself. All of the tasks you will be doing in your gardens, such as digging and pruning, are great for your body. They increase blood circulation and make your hands stronger. All that, while being an amazing experience!

Your friends will be amazed by how much you know about gardening and will want to learn more too. You could start your own gardening club or even consider cultivating certain plants for them.

All you have to do is become a neighborhood gardening expert!

Everyone will appreciate your knowledge and passion for gardening, so you will soon find yourself surrounded by people who love this hobby as much as you do.

After all, there's nothing better than a common interest that brings people together!

But, before you proceed, you must understand that gardens are not just places where you can grow your food. They are special spots that have to be nurtured with much care and thoughtfulness.

Now, since you know why it's good for the earth, your family, friends, and yourself, let us get into some fun activities!

Chapter 1: Gardening basics

I t might seem like an easy-to-do activity, but nothing could be further from the truth. There's a lot you need to learn before starting a garden, and this chapter will explain all of that. Soon enough, you'll become a green thumb everyone loves!

What does it mean to be a kid gardener?

We already discussed in the introduction what gardening is. But to be called a kid gardener, you must become a responsible, caring, and attentive person.

You must also know what plants need to grow well. Finally, remember that you can always get help if there's something you don't understand.

So, let's start with what plant needs?

A plant needs water, soil, sun, and air. The point is that regardless of the sort of plants you'll be cultivating, they will always require these three basic elements in addition to any other elements. Sunflowers, for example, can develop in almost any type of soil, but their blooms will be larger if the ground is well-nurtured.

On the other hand, if your flowers can't get enough sunlight, they will grow weak and be less attractive. But don't worry; you'll find out how to deal with any situation as you read on.

What is the best way to start your first garden?

Start with Location Hunting!

Before deciding what place is best for starting your garden, think about these things and make a note of your answers.

- **What do you want to grow?**
- **How much time do you plan to dedicate to gardening?**
- **What kind of garden style do you like?**

Now, depending on the size of your future garden, try thinking about these details you can use an adult's help as well:

- **Whether it's big or small?**
- **Is there enough sunlight for all the plants?**
- **Does the soil need improving to make it more suitable for growing?**
- **Does the garden have access to water?**

Once you've settled these details, you can start planning out your garden.

You can also pick a location in your house for gardening indoors. The only difference between indoor and outdoor gardens is that when it's cold outside or when there's not enough sunlight, you'll have to provide the right conditions for your plants yourself.

What are some common beginner gardening mistakes, and how to avoid them?

The first mistake people make when starting a garden is growing too many types of plants at once. That's why it's best to start with one or two kinds of flowers or vegetables. If you try to take care of all the plants at once, you'll just get confused about their needs, leading to failure.

The second thing beginners do wrong is not preparing the soil for growing. The soil can be too dry or too wet, and that's why it has to be improved before planting anything there. Wet soil is hard to improve, so sometimes it might be better to start the garden somewhere else.

The third thing to avoid is not giving your plants enough water or air. Some plants can grow in dry soil, but others need it to be moist at all times. Paying too much attention to one type of plant won't hurt, but you can easily forget about other things like water since you're busy with other plants.

Now that you know what a plant needs in order to grow, it's time for you to choose the perfect flower or vegetable type for your garden. After all, when starting out, you can't always make mistakes; this section will help you pick well!

What to plant?

A plant can grow either from seed or from a cutting. Seeds are usually smaller in size, but they take much longer to grow into plants.
On the other hand, cuttings are larger and easier to get started with. There are also other things like bulbs, tubers, and corms which are all different types of embryonic plants that start growing when you add water and go through the process of sprouting.

Plants can be divided into the following three categories-

> **Annuals**

These plants will thrive for a year, after which they will perish.; they are best for beginners or for people who don't have much time.

> **Biennials**

They take two seasons to mature, so it's better if you can dedicate the proper amount of time to them.

> **Perennials**

These plants last longer than the other two types, and they don't perish at the end of the season.

Plants from seeds

These plants can be started in a small container with soil, and you benefit from them when they're mature enough to be transplanted.

You should know that there are eight different types of seeds, which are Baby seeds, Creole seeds, Edible seeds, Flower seeds, Fruit seeds, Vegetable seeds, Hybrid seeds, Improved seeds.

- **Baby seeds-**

They're a type of seed that has been altered so that the plant stays little after it sprouts. The seeds are also excellent for eating since they're soft and tasty.

- **Creole seeds-**

They are indigenous seeds, which have not been modified, at least not artificially. This implies that they are the plants' natural offspring, harvested after their blooms were pollinated.

The greatest thing about them is that they adapt quickly to your region's conditions.

- **Edible seeds -**

These seeds can be eaten and, as a result, are produced for that purpose. There are many edible seeds: pistachios, walnuts, corn, oats, sesame, pumpkin, chia, rice, etc.

- **Flower seeds -**

Flower seeds come in a variety of shapes, sizes, and textures. That is why you must pick the best seedbed for them to have adequate room to grow.

- **Fruit seeds-**

There are many types of fruit seeds as there are many types of fruits. Mango, watermelon, apple, grape seed are just a few examples.

The majority of the time, the plants that produce them are grown in orchards; however, with sufficient space and knowledge, you can grow some of them in your garden as well.

- **Vegetable seeds-**

These seeds produce plants that are cultivated for their edible fruit, stem, leaf, flower, seed, and root. They all need constant humidity to germinate, as well as heat; therefore, they're sown in the spring.

- **Hybrid seeds-**

These seeds are developed by crossbreeding two different plants whose qualities are desired in the offspring plant. As a result, they might be more resilient, produce more fruits and seeds, and resist insects and illnesses.

- **Improved seeds -**

This category includes seeds cultivated by humans through a series of methods and processes in a controlled environment.

They have several advantages since they will sprout plants better adapted to the environment.

Plants that will be easier for beginners if grown from seed

Tomatoes- They can grow in all kinds of soil, and they don't need too much sunlight. You can also get seeds that are hybrids or heirlooms.

Carrots- They usually take around six weeks to start showing up in your garden, which makes them a great choice for anyone who doesn't have time to tend the garden every day.

Lettuce- it's good for growing in both containers and on open ground; it only takes two weeks to see results in your lettuce plants!

Flowers- like marigolds, nasturtiums, calendula, sunflowers, and pansies can grow from seeds, and they only need 5 to 6 weeks.

Herbs- like basil, thyme, sage, parsley, and lavender can all be grown from seeds.

Cucumbers- they're perfect for people who don't have much free time to care about the garden regularly since they can grow in just three weeks.

Plants that are easier to grow from cuttings

These types of plants are best grown using a cutting or a bulb instead of seeds. This is because they are larger and more mature when you get them, so it's easier to transplant them after getting them started. Plants from cuttings are bigger than seeds. They reproduce by rooting after you place them in the soil and water them regularly. There are four types of cuttings: Softwood cuttings, Herbaceous cuttings, Semi-hardwood cuttings, and Hardwood cuttings.

Plants that will be easier for beginners if grown from cuttings

Mint- All it takes is a 3-inch piece of stem, and it will grow roots within seven days. It does well in small pots as long as it receives enough sunlight (at least 4 hours per day).

Roses- these plants reproduce from cuttings that you take from a previous plant. You will need a strong stem, and it's best if the leaves are still attached to the cutting when you put them in the soil.

Lavender- it's best to plant them during the start of spring. You can take a 2-inch stem and plant it in a container filled with rich soil that is also well-drained.

Scented geraniums- 12 inches tall can be made from a cutting, which will need to have its leaves removed beforehand. They're perfect for containers or for growing indoors in pots that are exposed to lots of sunlight.

Pine trees- They can easily grow from cuttings because all you have to do is stick the cutting into some moist soil, wait for it to sprout roots, and then transplant it wherever you want.

Herbs- like basil, parsley, and thyme can all be grown from cuttings because they're perfect beginner plants; you only need one week before the roots will start to form!

How should I prepare the soil?

As mentioned before, there are different kinds of plants; each one requires specific care depending on the kind of soil needed to start growing properly. Therefore, knowing what type of soil your plant prefers is the key to a successful garden.

Plants that prefer sandy soil

These plants can grow well in dry and warm conditions, and they need plenty of sunlight, too. Some examples of plants like this include sunflowers, zinnias, annuals like poppies, dianthus, cornflower, and cosmos.

Plants that like loamy soil

They make great pets for those who don't have much time because they can grow really quickly; some examples are foxgloves, snapdragons, carn (you should place them in moist soil), and campanulas (they can grow in cooler conditions).

Plants that prefer clay soil

These plants should be planted in full sunlight, and they should also have a constant supply of water so that their roots can grow properly. You can choose annuals like a wallflower, pansy, primrose, bee balm, and sweet pea; perennials include lavender and chrysanthemum.

Salt tolerant plants

They should be planted away from the sea because they need fresh water. When you buy them from the market, look for the ones marked as salt-tolerant to make sure that your garden will be great no matter where it's situated. Some examples are tomatoes (they need plenty of moisture) and petunias (they grow in small spaces).

Plants that, can tolerate dry weather

These seeds should be planted close to the ground, but they should also be left in moist conditions; some examples are poppies, cornflower, evening primrose, and foxglove.

By following these simple steps and choosing the right plant for the right type of soil, you'll be able to enjoy a successful garden filled with gorgeous flowers and vegetables!

Before that, let's dive deep into understanding the tools you would require to work on gardening.

Know your tools and materials required for gardening

Pots

To start gardening, you will need some pots. Depending on the size of your plant, you can choose a small pot or a big one; make sure that it has room for growth because if the soil becomes too dry, then the roots won't be able to grow properly, and they might end up dying!

Seeds or cuttings

As discussed before, not all plants need to be grown from seeds. You can also grow a plant from a cutting! Choose your desired type.

Watering can

This will help to keep your garden moist, especially if you're planting flowers or vegetables. Make sure that you water them daily so that they can develop strong roots!

Compost

Compost is made from organic waste, manure, or other material that can make the soil richer. Manure comes in many different varieties, and you can choose the one that fits your garden best! It's very important to make compost early on because it will be used as the plant's food source.

Soil for indoor plants

When you buy soil for indoor plants, make sure that there's little or no sand in it; even though this type of soil is really good for growing most types of plants, if your plant prefers sandy soil, then mix some organic matter into the potting mix before planting.

Tape measure

For measuring out how much soil you will need.

Plant labels

These are a great way of keeping track of your garden and a fun way to mark the plants you have there.

Hoe

A hoe makes it easier to work with your soil and evens out hard dirt so that the roots can spread more quickly.

Gardening gloves

To protect your hands from dirt and bugs, it's a good idea to wear gardening gloves. When choosing them, keep in mind that heavy-duty ones are best for shrubs or for handling spiky plants. To protect your hands from dirt and bugs, wear some gardening gloves.

Garden fork

Also known as an "awl," this tool is used to dig holes for seeds of new cuttings; you can choose how big the hole should be depending on the size of the plant!

Trowel

This item is a smaller version of a garden fork used to dig small holes and also for weeding.

Spray bottle

The process of spraying non-chemical pesticides such as soap, oil, or vinegar solution (1 teaspoon in 1-liter water) will help the plants develop their natural defenses against pests without harming them. Keep in mind that organic methods take longer, but they are ultimately better for your plants and garden.

Spade

You'll need it for cutting back roots and mixing compost into the soil.

Rake

This tool is mainly used only in the garden, so you should use it if there are some dead leaves on the ground, stones, etc.

Sieves

They're used in order to separate the lighter gravels from the heavier soil in your garden. You can also sift organic matter if needed!

Pruning shears

These are useful when you need to prune bushes or trees. You can buy them in different sizes depending on how big or small your project is.

A fork

Garden forks are used for turning over the soil and breaking up larger clumps of dirt. You should buy a lightweight one because it will be easier to use when working in smaller spaces.

Wheelbarrow

This is perfect if you don't want to carry loads of dirt on your own; wheelbarrows allow easy transportation of materials without straining yourself too much!

Gardening scissors

They are used for cutting away dead plant materials, cutting twine, and so on. This tool is also handy for picking up fallen leaves or even pinecones!

Gardening Diary

Keep track of your garden projects so that you can keep improving them!

These tools will help you weed your garden and prepare the soil for planting. They're really simple to use; you just need to push them into the earth and pull out the weeds. Keep in mind that you should wear gloves because some of these tools can be sharp!

Now that you know your tools and have your favorite plant ready for planting, it's time to take care of it! In the next chapter, you'll read about what to do each day as a gardener. It's as easy as one-two-three once you get the hang of it!

Chapter 2- Getting started

The practical work requires good preparation and a bit of effort. Your garden prompts you to get your hands dirty but also gives rewards! I will help you through the step-by-step process. If you do everything right, the reward is tasty fruit and veggies for you and your family.

All you need is to take care of your plants, and they will be very happy!

Every day is different, but there are some things that you need to do regularly.

But, before getting started with practical work, remember the most important thing is safety.

So, **Safety first!**

Here're the safety guidelines you must follow while gardening-

Thoroughly examine your site of the garden

Take the help of adults and inspect the area for any poisonous plants or insects and take notes of their location in your gardening diary. Ensure that the soil is not contaminated with harmful chemicals or septic waste and take care to avoid such hazards.

Choose a safe source of water

Your municipal water is usually a safe bet. Irrigate your edible garden with a potable water source. Have the water you're using tested for bacterial and other sorts of contamination on a regular basis if it comes from a private well or an untreated surface water source, such as a pond or river.

Your local health department can help you locate testing facilities.

Do not use chemicals

Never use harsh chemicals as you might harm yourself. Always try natural ways for fertilizers and pesticides. You can easily make it at home by the following method-

Mix 1 teaspoon of salt in a liter of water and put it into a spray bottle; mix the same amount of baking soda with two teaspoons of dishwashing soap and vinegar (use white vinegar as it's acidic). Spray this solution on your plants as this will stop pests from eating their leaves!

Choose the appropriate tools

Handle them with care to avoid injuries. Since hand power is used, it's important that the tool is lightweight enough so that you can work comfortably without hurting yourself. Wearing gardening gloves made from sturdy material is recommended while using tools. Sharp objects such as secateurs for pruning shears should be used under adult supervision, and you must remember to put them back on the shelf after use.

Remember

Do not leave your tools out in the rain or sunshine, as it can cause rusting and eventually damage them. Take good care of your garden tools so that they last longer!

Be extra vigilant with manure

Even though manure is a natural fertilizer, it can have pathogens in it, which can cause you to get sick. It is best to apply manure around established plants in the fall, as they are less susceptible to infection. Always use gloves when you are working with any fertilizer or manure.

Always have adult supervision

Most of these activities are simple enough, but you should not forget that there are chances of injuries because of the tools involved. So, always have a person who is more experienced or aged supervise when you are gardening.

Dress properly

Wear long pants, closed shoes, and gloves while gardening. You'll need to protect your hands from dirt or bug bites! You can also wear insect repellent or citronella oil which is very effective but try not to use it too much because it can be harmful to plants. Wear hats and sunscreen to avoid sunburns.

Personal hygiene

Remove all clothes after gardening and take a bath. Wash your hands regularly when you are gardening. Don't eat or drink with dirty hands! Clean your clothes worn during gardening.

Know when not to garden

If you are sick, do not go near your plants. If you are taking medicine, consult with your doctor if it is safe for gardening before you begin. Health always comes first! Also, don't work outside if the climate is too harsh; listen to your adults when they refrain you from gardening.

Follow your parent/carer's advice

Gardening is a wonderful hobby, but you should always listen to adults. They have done this before, and they can guide you with proper methods.

Be safe!

Always read the instructions on the product label before using it on your plants or in your garden! Gardening can be fun for all ages; just be sure to prioritize safety over everything else!

Now that you know all about gardening safety precautions. Let's dive to,

A practical guide for planting.

First of all, check the daily forecast and plan accordingly.

You can grow plants at any time in a year but remember that certain veggies have the preferred season. When the weather is favorable, start with pruning- it helps in the better growth of shoots and fruits or vegetables.

In summer, weed out the garden so that its roots don't disturb crops. Check the soil frequently to ensure they're moist enough but not wet enough. Finally, keep inspecting for pests on a regular basis!

Time to plant

As you know all your tools and gardening information, you can start planting. Choose the type of plant you want to grow and research their specific requirements; use the information provided in the first chapter. The number of plants depends upon how much sun or shade they need. Follow the guidelines that come along with the seeds; it's important to be precise!

Plant them at the right depth and space, depending upon their development needs. Dig a hole in the middle of each pot or on the ground with an appropriate depth. Fill the hole with soil mixed with manure or compost for fertilizing your plants.

Start small as they can get big over time.

Mix fertilizers after reading instructions

Mix fertilizer with water according to the instructions on the packet. Pour this mixture at the base or root of your plants or vegetables/ crops very gently, never directly! You can use compost tea for better growth results.

Water regularly

Maintain humidity levels around the soil by watering them daily- not too much or too little! It's easier to prevent weeds than to remove them after growing, so make sure you weed out every week or whenever needed. Watering helps in the removal of dead tissues from vegetables/ crops, so water is very necessary for growth.

Remove weeds when you see them

Weeds are unwanted plants that can inhibit growth or spread diseases to your crops. Whenever you see them, remove them by pulling the roots gently so as not to damage nearby plants.

Check that plant is getting enough sunlight

Regularly check that crops are getting enough sunlight. They need at least 6-8 hours of sun every day to grow well! For indoor plants, you need to be extra cautious! In case they're not getting enough sunlight, you can place them in a sunny window or near a bright light.

Stay positive and be patient!

Stressing about gardening is not going to help, so keep a positive attitude and enjoy the process of making your backyard garden better. Growing veggies or plants take time, effort, and patience that will all lead up to a wonderful end product! Never lose hope if a plant does not yield as expected because there's always something good around the corner!

Are you ready for harvesting? Bring in your harvest by storing them the right way!

Harvesting

To harvest veggies like cabbages, cauliflower, and broccoli, cut off their florets or flowers, respectively. Cut plants near the base so the plant itself can regrow next season! You

should shear vegetables like carrots or radishes instead of cutting them as they tend to recover quickly, unlike others.

Harvest fruits like grapes, berries, etc., after their color change from green to bright yellow/orange/red, which means they're fully ripe and ready to eat!

Pick fruits and vegetables when they're ripe

Harvest them before the ground freezes, or it may rot. You can check the soil temperature to know if frost is coming. Place harvested vegetables/fruits in a cool and dry place like a basement, shed, etc., where humidity levels are low and ideal for storing veggies!

Store apples, stone fruits, and other fruit by laying them on a table covered with newspaper sheets. Grains should be stored in an airtight container which you can buy from any home improvement store.

Remember that excess moisture should be avoided while storing veggies as it causes rotting. Be patient till the next growing season! The best time to start gardening is directly after winter ends, which means it's time to plant new crops again!

Now that you know the overall process let's make a weekly routine to help you plan better once the initial planting is done.

Days of the week and time to work in your garden

You can follow these instructions for each day of the week:

Monday: Weeding and pruning

On Monday, it's time to get started with weeding and pruning. Weeds absorb nutrients from the soil, which can harm your plants, so remove them as soon as possible! Cut branches or stems at the base instead of pulling them out by their leaves so that the plant remains intact. You can also use a sharp spade or hoe to cut through weeds easily.

Tuesday: Planting new crops/seeds

Seeds are available in packets that come with complete instructions on how to plant them. You can sow seeds directly into the ground or start them indoors. Make sure you know your area before planting new plants!

Wednesday: Fertilizing and harvesting

Water your plants every day so that the soil is moist enough for good growth! It's time to feed plants with fertilizer if required; watermelon requires lots of nutrients, so apply compost at the base of its stem every week after it starts flowering. Finally, harvesting time comes, which means gently removing vegetables/fruits from their stem or roots respectively. Remember not to damage nearby plants while harvesting!

Thursday: Make compost

Composting is necessary if you want to make your soil nutrient rich. To learn how to make compost, you should refer to these instructions carefully-

1- First, you need to collect all the compostable materials in your house like eggshells, burnt toast, etc. Please make sure they're dry but not too dry!

2- Next, put these compostable materials in a bucket or bin with holes at the bottom so air can pass through easily. Add water if necessary, during this process! You can add dried leaves or grass clippings for better results.

3- Then, cover the bin/bucket with a lid and leave it outside in direct sunlight for several weeks. This way, bacteria inside create heat that is required to break down items into rich soil!

4- Finally, when everything breaks down into thick black matter, then it's ready to use in your garden.

Friday: Protect plants against pests and diseases

Pests like aphids or snails attack plants by sucking out their nutrients which leads to wilting of leaves and other problems. Plant disease can be prevented by spraying them with fungicides! You can find many organic solutions at hardware stores, so check there first for fungicides before buying one online!

Saturday: Relax and enjoy the fruits of your labor

After each week comes to an end, take some time to relax and enjoy what you've accomplished so far. You can visit your plants daily, look at the weather and anticipate the upcoming week's plan!

Sunday: Go shopping and rest

It's time to go shopping for new gardening supplies like tools, saplings, etc., if required. Remember that low prices should always be preferred as expensive items don't necessarily provide better results than cheap ones.

And you deserve some time to relax with your family and friends. You can enjoy your meal or just sit around in the garden during this day- it's up to you!

Apart from this, some things should be done regularly,

What to do each day as a gardener

Keep an eye on plants and trees. Ensure that all your plants are healthy and safe for gardening. Plant any seeds or bulbs you see! Maintain records of what you planted, when they were planted, and where. All this information can be helpful later when you decide to harvest them.

Keep the surrounding areas clean and remove damaged leaves and branches as soon as possible. Trash can be used, but don't burn them as they release toxic gases! If you see weeds, pull them out carefully by their roots.

Water your plants at least once a day to make sure the soil is moist enough for good growth. It is also important not to let too many nutrients run away with water runoff or accumulate in the form of fertilizer or manure salt deposits at the base of plants, known as fertilizer burn.

I am sure by now you must have understood how to be a gardener and must have enjoyed learning about it!

As we become master gardeners, let's move towards creating beautiful theme gardens. The next chapter will help you create a beautiful garden with themes that you wish to have!

It's time to surprise people with your creativity!

Chapter 3: Theme Gardening

Theme gardens are a type of gardening that allows you to create a garden with a certain theme of your choice. A themed garden can be made by adding essential components like plants, sculptures, statues, rest-houses, waterfalls, ponds, fountains, and ponds.

Theme gardens not only look beautiful but also provide you with a serene environment in your backyard or garden, perfect for relaxation and outings!

Before creating a themed garden, first select the theme of your choice, whether it's indoor or outdoor! Then, considering your space available, you can plan how much area is required for each component.

For example, if you want to create an indoor garden, you have more control over where plants are placed because the size of indoor spaces is limited, unlike outdoor gardens with vast areas without boundaries. Therefore, designing an indoor garden will require more thought and planning than that of an outdoor one!

However, even if it's designed well, be ready for some required maintenance for indoor gardens as they need proper sunlight, so plants don't die easily. Compared to this, the maintenance of an outdoor theme garden needs less than anything that fits the theme. The best part about the themed garden is that it makes your garden look like a one of a kind!

Theme gardens can be created for different themes depending on the person making them and their interests.
I will share some of my favorite ones-

Fairy Gardening theme

Aesthetic: This theme is suitable for all weather conditions and can be placed anywhere indoors or outdoors.

Plants: Tiny-looking plants like ferns, lavenders, baby's tears, etc., are good for this themed garden as they look fairy-like!

Decorations: Look for tiny pots, thrones, maybe some colored butterflies to decorate the garden.

Process: Ensure that the space available is near a window or if you want it to be indoor, place it in any corner of your house. Create a square or rectangular-shaped garden and start planting flowers. Use stakes to give support if required. Put tiny pots at 4 points, where the square meets diagonally, and finally decorate with small thrones.

In addition, you can add small cottages, pagodas, or houses made of natural materials like wood and stones with some tiny furniture inside. Small plants are required for this themed garden as they look perfect in these kinds of gardens. To decorate the garden, use small pots, tables, and chairs at different points, or even a small pond can be added if space allows. Decorate with tiny boxes and colorful butterflies!

What to expect: A fairy garden will make your house look like a home of little fairies or people who wish to live in one!

Play Gardening Theme

Aesthetic: This theme is suitable if you like playing in your garden. The garden can be created anywhere, indoor or outdoor, and is good for all weather conditions.

Plants: Depending upon the kind of play you want your garden to look like, select the plants accordingly. For example, if it's a playhouse, then you can use small flowers with some grasses! On the other hand, if it's an adventure-themed kid play garden, use wildflowers with small trees! Choose fast-growing plants, vines, creepers, etc., for this theme. You can also use edible plants that are relatively faster growing, like strawberry, corn, etc., along with some lovely flowers that are brightly colored!

Decorations: Sculptures look perfect in play gardening themed gardens. They can range from small to large depending on the space available. Apart from sculptures, you can also add swings or seesaws or even a see-saw table! You could also make art forms of animals using recycled materials like clay pots, toys, etc. if you wish to do so.

Process: Start by giving your ideal shape to the garden, whether it is circular, triangular, rectangular, or any other. Once you have given your shape, start adding edible plants as they grow fast and keep the garden looking fresh all year round! Then add some flowers according to your chosen theme and finally place a plant of choice where the path leads. Leave a good amount of space for the play activities to take place.

What to expect: A play gardening themed garden will bring out your adventurous side, making you live life on the edge.

Butterfly Gardening Theme

Aesthetic: This theme is suitable if you like butterflies and will look perfect when placed outside.

Plants: Only plants that attract butterflies should be used in this themed garden because the sole purpose of this themed garden is to provide a habitat for butterflies! So avoid using plants like vegetables or corn in the butterfly-themed garden. You can choose from a range of colorful flowers that attract butterflies. Some safe places to add them are- Hibiscus, Sunflower, Marigold, etc.! Not just flowers, even some other plants like water lilies and grasses look fabulous along with these beautiful flowers!

Decorations: Statues like fairies, gnomes, butterflies are perfect for this theme. Add them wherever you can! Also, add houses, benches, etc., where butterflies may land on!

Process: This theme requires a lot of patience as you cannot simply create your garden overnight or in one day. Start by creating habitats like piles of leaves, flower pots with some grass and leaves on them, logs, etc. You can also create your own habitats for butterflies! Plant some flowers that attract butterflies and wait for a few weeks. Once the plants start growing and look healthy, add some more of such plants. Your garden is ready when you see butterflies fluttering around!

What to expect: A butterfly-themed garden will attract lots of beautiful butterflies, which will make your garden look like a place of magic.

Shoe Gardening Theme

Aesthetic: This is my favorite theme as it makes gardening very interesting for kids and adults alike! Themed gardens can be created anywhere indoor or outdoor and are good for all weather conditions. It gives boho vibes to your garden, making it look unique and quirky! It's a space-saving theme and can be created in any corner of your house. This themed garden is good for all weather conditions.

Plants: Use small to medium-sized plants in your themed garden. You can use climbers or creepers for decorating purposes. Fill in any gaps with grasses and wildflowers too. For this themed garden, choose small flowering plants that suit your shoes/boots size.

Suited plants for this themed garden are those which create perforated leaves like parlor palms, rubber plants, etc., as they look like shoes!

Decorations: Look for polished stones, tiny pots, thrones, maybe some colored butterflies to decorate the garden. Remember, not all gardens need a lot of decoration as they give a natural vibe! On the other hand, if you wish to make your theme stand out, then do add some extra flair using figurines, doors, etc., along with plant lighting at nighttime!

Process: The only thing that's important while creating a shoe-themed garden is making sure the plants selected are small and can easily be placed in pots/containers. The containers used should be of all shapes and sizes. You may even add some broken pottery or ornamentation like tiny boots, shoes, etc., or any other creative idea of your choice!

What to expect: A shoe-themed garden will give your home a boho vibe along with making you feel creative inside out.

Tropical porch Gardening Theme

Aesthetic: This theme is perfect for outdoor summers and is unique due to the tropical plants added to it! There's nothing more refreshing than enjoying an evening on your porch with a cooling breeze! This theme requires a large open space as it will give you lots of options to decorate the garden.

Plants: Use small-sized plants/shrubs which can give an amazing feel to your porch! Fill any gaps using grasses and flowers too! For this theme, avoid using big plants as they generally take up all the space! Some safe plants for this theme are- Pothos, Heartleaf Philodendron, Fiddle Leaf Fig, etc.

Decorations: For this themed garden, create its own unique decorations like colored ferns, spiky plant spikes, etc. You may also use some other accessories like water features along with plant lighting for an evening delight! In addition, add some extra porch swing or hammocks to make your porch feel even more luxurious!

Process: To start this themed garden, ensure you have an open space. Then create two partitions using palm trees planted in large pots with slow-growing plants/shrubs on the sides. This will give a perfect tropical vibe to your garden. You may plant some vine flowers along with small grasses for decoration purposes too! Remember to always place the big plants at the center while placing smaller ones on the sides!

What to expect: A tropical porch garden will fill you up with freshness, and its bright colors will lighten up your mood instantly! Plant lighting at night time adds a magical feel to it, making you forget all worries of life!

Mini pizza gardening Theme

Aesthetic: This theme is perfect for all seasons and is unique due to the mix of veggies, fruits, etc. In this themed garden, use decorative pizza slices as a partition and plant ingredients of pizza. The best thing about this themed garden is that it can be created indoors as well as outdoors making it a versatile theme!

Plants: You can use veggies, herbs, and fruits used in pizza-like bell peppers, basil, etc. Fill any gaps using grasses and flowers too! For this garden, choose small size plants that look like toppings on your pizzas! Some safe plants apart from pizza ingredients for this themed garden are- Aloe Vera, Coleus, Miniature rose, etc.

Decorations: Creating unique decorations is the key to making a mini pizza-themed garden stand out. Try adding figurines of veggies, cheese slicer, knife, pizza cutter, which will make your garden unique in itself. You may also add some other accessories like tiny pots with herbs used in pizza or miniature pizza slice statues along with plant lighting for an evening delight!

Look for some statues or figurines to give an artistically appealing look to this theme. Decorative items like pots in different colors with matching plant labels make your garden look attractive.

Process: For this themed garden, you will need a partition that can be made using decorative pizza slices planted in pots/containers. Make sure that you place taller plants on one side while placing smaller ones on the sides! If there are any gaps, plant grasses or flowers to fill them. Fill in with some colorful butterflies and accessory stones like a heart-shaped paw print, etc., for added attraction.

What to expect: Mini pizza-themed garden will give your home a modern feel along with making you feel fresh inside out! Add some pizzazz to this theme by using decorative items like colored pots etc. A mini pizza-themed garden will instantly give a true Italian pizzeria feel to your home as all the ingredients will be fresh!

Potato time tower Theme

Aesthetic: This is perfect for all seasons with its good cultivation rate! Create a tower of hay along with some decorative stones to make your garden stand out. Plant vines at the base of the tower.

Plants: Potatoes, ornamental grasses, colorful flowers.

Decorations: Add some small ornaments like rocks or figurines or other such creative things to add interest to the theme. Use plant lighting during the nighttime if you wish to illuminate your head! Fill in gaps with moss and stones to give your themed garden a natural feel.

Process: Find potatoes that have healthier skins since these will be more durable than their sprouting counterparts. After that, construct your tower. Cover the potatoes with about a foot of hay and dirt mixed together by lining the tower's edges with hay. You must maintain your potato crop covered, or you'll grow green, poisonous potatoes as it grows. Because the structure is more exposed to the air, keep it well-watered throughout the growing season. You can use a few cute containers to create a tower instead of using hay. You can also use decorative stones or any other creative things you wish to add interest to your garden.

What to Expect: Potato time tower-themed garden will give you fresh potatoes along with the opportunity to show your creativity! Decorate this theme with colorful pots and vines at the base. A potato time tower garden will make sure that your mood is instantly lifted!

All the theme gardens are beautiful if you put effort and creativity into them. Experiment as much as you like, and don't be afraid to use your imagination. You can try different themes and see which one suits your space and mood!

Take help from any one of your family members or friends if you need it. Just make sure that you ask them for advice and not their whole time; you must do it yourself.

A garden like this will help you grow even more artistic with your creativity and imagination. It will enhance your skills and give you one more reason to love gardening.

So, go ahead and plan your own garden or themed garden to enhance your inner green thumb!

I hope you have selected your theme, and let's start your green garden!

Chapter 4: Green Garden

Green gardening is all about using sustainable practices to produce food. It can also be defined as a system of agriculture that takes care of the environment and soil fertility.

You have to use natural fertilizers or compost from your own leaf litter and garden waste rather than chemical fertilizers in this kind of gardening. Using a good organic mulch at the base of plants is also a very important green gardening practice for retaining moisture in the soil and preventing weeds from growing around cultivated plants.

Green gardeners believe that only healthy soils support healthy plants, which ultimately provide high-quality, healthy food products that are free from chemicals sprayed on them.

When you start with green gardening, there is no end to it; it's an ongoing process that needs constant attention, especially until you get to the point where you don't have to keep checking on your plants every day.
You might be thinking,

Why prefer Green gardening?

Green gardening has multiple benefits for both the environment and the people eating the food produced.

Environmental benefits of Green gardening are:

• Biodiversity thrives in a garden where chemical pesticides are not used, meaning that you have more insects, birds, butterflies, and other wildlife in your green garden, which can positively affect our ecosystem.

• Pesticides release toxic chemicals into the air while green gardeners use mulches which retain moisture in the soil and keep it cool, stopping evaporation. They also help heat up soil at lower levels so plants can grow well, even during winter.

• Chemical fertilizers are harmful to bees because they are attracted to them, making plants produce pollen with altered DNA, linked to collapse disorder (CCD)in bees. Green gardens don't use any kind of chemicals, and so there is no danger of pollen with altered DNA being produced.

• Chemical fertilizers contain salts that accumulate in the soil as dead spots that can become difficult to grow anything on these areas later on as they don't retain water and nutrients effectively.

• Organic matter such as compost, leaf litter, and mulch eventually break down into humus, providing a natural source of nutrients for plants instead of chemical fertilizers.

The Health benefits of green gardening are:

• The food we eat from a green garden is pesticide-free and has great taste because it's not sprayed with chemicals during its growing period or after harvesting, as only the nutrient-rich organic matter was used to maintain its growth.

• Food from a green garden is free from chemicals and is also more nutritious as it has been grown using organic fertilizers, which provide additional nutrients to the plants.

• Chemical fertilizers often contain high levels of nitrates which can be hazardous for human health too if consumed in high amounts. However, organic matter does not cause the accumulation of nitrates in the soil, so there's no chance of consuming something harmful for our bodies.

Now that we know its importance, let's learn how you can create your own green garden.

How to create your green garden?

You can create your green garden by using mulch made out of coconut husk, cocoa shells, composted leaves, and other waste products. This will ensure that nutrients are re-used in the soil while keeping weeds away.

Using organic fertilizers is another great way you can go green when gardening. In addition, regularly adding layers of leaf litter at the base of growing plants is a great way to recycle organic wastes.

You could also make your own compost bin or container to recycle your kitchen waste into high-quality fertilizer, which you could spread around among all your plants!

These are some simple ways to start going green with your gardening, and soon, you will start seeing the results with your own eyes!

Here's a step-wise process of creating a green garden-

1) Dig a small pit and place some coconut husk and cocoa shells in it.

2) Place this container wherever you find space, preferably near the plants that need care more often, such as tomatoes or potatoes.

3) Cover this with leaves and add another layer on top every few days to create layers of mulch.

4) Add kitchen wastes such as vegetable peels, eggshells, etc., between these layers. This will help all the organic matter to decompose quickly into humus which is beneficial for plants.

5) Use organic fertilizers made at home using ingredients mentioned earlier in the article to fertilize your plants during their growing period. This will ensure that they are getting nutrients from an organic source rather than chemicals.

6) Save money while shopping at home by using the seeds you get from your harvest or even use saved seeds from previous harvests if they are still feasible!

7) Rotate your crops every year while growing things together that fix nitrogen into the soil, creating almost no need for any added nitrogen fertilizers!

8) Use a variety of plants so in case certain kinds don't do well in a particular season, other kinds will take over in their place without requiring any further work from you since they all have different needs!

9) Harvest your veggies and fruits when they are ready to eat! These will taste much better than vegetables and fruits from the supermarket because you don't need to worry about any chemicals since you used natural fertilizers throughout their growth period.

10) Have fun while gardening and learn about environmental impact, healthy eating habits, and growing food at an early age!

You will soon have a green garden to love and cherish as you become clear about the green gardening process. But, to achieve it even more easily,

Avoid these common mistakes as a green gardener:

- Avoid using chemicals to produce food that can harm you and the environment!
- Not recycling waste products around your plants.
- Avoid gardening in a space without providing water for plants at regular intervals.
- Not reading up on different types of fertilizers which can be used as per plant requirements.
- Constructing a garden where rainwater cannot reach it easily.
- Allowing yourself to get overwhelmed by trying to go green all at once instead of taking small steps towards it at regular intervals.
- Forgetting about mulching and using specific fertilizers with desired nutrients for healthier plants and soil! (Remember: "Prevention is better than cure")
- Not thinking about the weather conditions before planting specific plants as some of them require a lot of Sun while some others need shade.
- Not doing enough research about organic fertilizers and their availability in local markets near you!
- Using too much or too little water- can be harmful to soil and plants.
- Not using mulch regularly to build a sustainable green garden.
- Planting new grass on top of existing soil where there is no grass growth which will result in dead spots forming with time! Remember: "Grass helps clean up certain toxins."

- Not supporting local nurseries and shops that sell organic fertilizers, composts, or other types of mulch/mixtures helps create a sustainable green garden.
- Not providing enough shade for your plants to survive during the summer months.
- Not re-using existing mulch or leaves/plant material that is decaying into compost.

As you progress with your sustainable green garden, you can add decoration and use terracotta pots or containers of different shapes and sizes to create a wonderful piece of art for yourself.

Your creativity knows no bounds when it comes to gardening so let's see what you can create for yourself.

Meanwhile, let's have a look at my favorite garden arts.

Chapter 5: Garden Art

There are many kinds of garden art that you can make to decorate your theme or green gardens. Your garden art can be as simple as a couple of pots and planters with vines and plants running down the side, or it can also be complex, like a furniture piece you would like to use for your seating!

Both kinds will make your gardens look prettier and will help you express yourself better. You can paint or draw anything that inspires you, even people's faces if that is what you wish for.

For example, if you like birds or any animal, in particular, paint their images on your pots and planters. Your imagination is the only thing standing between you and your garden art!

So go ahead and begin making your garden art, starting with things that are easily available at home. Then, you can either paint them yourself or ask someone else who has a good painting hand to do it for you – no matter what happens, your garden art will surely look pretty.

How to Make Garden Art?

Making simple garden arts like pots decorated with vines and plants is not as hard as it seems; all you need is a little bit of creativity and effort. As long as the piece has some relevance to gardening, go ahead and experiment!

Here is a list of some interesting garden arts and crafts which I love; along with methods to create them:

1. Hanging Planter

Use hangers to attach empty glass jars with the help of strings so they don't fall on the ground. Place them in different corners of your garden space but make sure to place them at least 1 foot apart because the idea behind this art is for each jar to produce its fresh herbs or vegetables independently without having any competition between plants!

2. Horse Stable Herb Garden

This is probably a unique type of garden art out there! If you have a space where you can place it, this is something you should try. It's also perfect if your theme happens to be western or has horses playing an important role in it. You can even use old buggy wheels and other rustic elements to make this piece of garden art, which will look very interesting once the plants are done growing around them!

3. Doll/Toy Art

Another terrific idea for garden arts and crafts is attaching toys to planters with the help of hangers so that they don't fall below. Toys like dollhouses, teddy bears, etc., look adorable when hung up on hangers attached to different parts of your garden space.

4. Animal Figures

You can attach animal figures with the help of hangers to planters or pots in your garden to make it look attractive! Animals like frogs, turtles, etc., are very cute and will definitely make an interesting outdoor art piece for your gardens. You can even paint their images on your garden's sidewalls if you have enough space to do so.

5. Flags/Flags Art

Flags will be a great idea for outdoor arts and crafts if your theme is about countries or sports. You can choose flags that represent different countries or teams that influence the theme of your green space, so it becomes more celebratory when needed! Make sure this art piece also has plants growing around it because happy plants make happy gardens!

6. Human Art

This is another very interesting garden art idea for creative people with a green thumb. You can use old wooden crates or pieces of paper and draw images of children on them, which you then cut out. Now, these mini images should be attached to empty jars that will serve as planters with vines growing around them! This way, your images grow progressively into more complex forms thanks to the plant life surrounding them. Finally, they become what they love to do most – gardening!

7. Recycled Bottle Herb Garden

Old, recycled bottles are among the best things you can use for making garden arts and crafts because they're so easy to find around us. You just need to cut off their bottoms then place them upside down into soil-filled pots or flower beds. Once they start sprouting, plant herbs inside of them like rosemary, basil, fennel, parsley, etc. Just pick the ones that grow well inside small spaces like this one!

8. Bicycle Tire Planters

Bicycle tire wheels are one of those garden arts and crafts ideas that take up little space but pack a lot of charm once they're done making them. You only need two bicycle tires per piece which you then hang from raised structures like beams or boards attached to the side of your garden walls. You can then plant seeds among them and watch as they grow into a beautiful green, flowery piece of garden art!

9. Rustic Garden Signpost

Making garden arts and crafts from new items is fun but recycling old stuff is even more interesting. That's why this rustic signpost idea might be one you need if you have a lot of materials lying around at home that could be restored to become part of your outdoor arts and crafts collection. All you need here is an old wooden board with metal plates on which you can attach letters that say different friendly messages for passers-by – things like "Welcome," "Garden Rules," "Don't touch the plants," etc.

10. Flower Painting

If you're a big fan of paintings and arts in general, this flower painting idea might be your thing. You obviously don't need to paint a whole garden wall for this purpose but small portions or spaces here, and there will do just fine. Just create paintings yourself that have flowers growing around them, so the piece becomes more vibrant when it comes to color! Your creations can look similar to modern art if you want to meet both old-school traditions and new-age concepts at once!

11. Vintage Treasure Boxes

Old vintage treasure boxes are an ideal addition to any garden that's colorful enough because they have their unique charm. They become part of the overall aesthetics, especially if they're made from metal with little keyholes on them! In addition, you can plant different flowers or herbs that grow into pots then put them on top of the treasure boxes, so they bloom nicely when an onlooker approaches.

12. Monochrome Checkered Garden Wall

This garden art idea is all about making your green space look more fun and modern. All you need is to get a huge, checkered piece of paper, preferably cut out from cardboard because it's durable enough for this purpose! Now, paint the whole thing using black-and-white colors so that one side has painted squares while the other simply remains white. Once it dries up, attach the thing to your garden walls with adhesive materials like glue or double-sided tapes. Then watch as passers-by stare at it with curiosity!

13. Garden Flags

Garden flags are among those arts and crafts ideas that take up little space but have a tremendous impact! All you need is to paint different drawings on different fabrics – one of which must be waterproof if possible – then stick them onto sticks or wooden poles that you stick into the soil right next to your plants. They'll start being flapped by wind, giving your garden an even more lively look!

14. Tin Can Planters

If you're still not getting enough from these easy arts and crafts ideas, this garden tutorial will be perfect for you because it involves tin cans! All you need are some big metal containers which you can easily cut in half with scissors before making holes on their lower sides.

Once all of them are ready, put soil inside them, then plant whatever seeds or seedlings that grow well into small spaces. You can paint the cans in different colors if you like, making them stand out even more!

15. Hanging Garden Baskets

This garden art idea is one of those that involve both creativity and simplicity at once. All you need are some big metal baskets which you can easily find in junk shops or simply make yourself by covering up wire mesh with fabric. Then, put soil inside them before hanging them on trees or walls around your garden, so they act as containers for plants like ivy. Another version of this idea is to plant all kinds of climbers on thick ropes to create a vine-like system that entirely covers an old wooden beam above your outdoor space.

16. Reclaimed Window Planting Boxes

Remember how we told you that you could find all kinds of interesting materials in junk shops? That's definitely the case with these window planting boxes! All you need is to place old windows on their backs then cut small holes around them. Once they're ready, plant different seedlings inside before hanging them from walls or fences using thick rope or chains. The best thing about this idea is that it looks incredibly stylish and will even be a great addition to your porch's look!

17. Hanging Pot Garden

Liven up your garden by adding several large metal pots filled with soil and different plants! All you need are some sturdy chains or ropes along with hooks. Attach them to either side of your garden's fence, making sure each one is in the middle, so they don't touch the ground! Also, make sure to use non-toxic paint so that all of these details won't be dangerous for anyone who goes inside the yard.

18. Painted Wheelbarrow

When it comes to backyard garden arts and crafts ideas, this one is definitely among the unique ones because it involves an old wheelbarrow that can be painted in various colors. Once done, fill its tray soil, then plant flowers or herbs inside it before pushing it around your outdoor space. If you don't have a wheelbarrow, this idea can obviously be adapted to a regular cart or a suitcase instead.

19. Personalized Art

Are you looking for more unique garden arts and crafts ideas? Well, these personalized pots are what you were looking for! All you need is to use old containers – plastic bottles work great here – then give them personal touches by writing names on them using paint or stickers. Plant whatever seedlings or small plants that grow well near the soil surface before hanging each pot from walls, doors, or fences with adhesive tapes. This will all liven up your garden incredibly!

20. Hidden Treasures

Here's one more idea for those looking for backyard decorating ideas: make small hidden treasures with different layers containing soil and plants inside them! These will look great along fences since they're nicely hidden from view when you're outside! Simply place old boxes or containers on their sides, cut small holes in them then plant different flowers and seeds inside before covering the top with soil.

21. DIY garden wind chimes

Turn old spoons into beautiful garden wind chimes in just a few easy steps. You'll need some silver spray paint, rope, and some old spoons with their edges filed down to avoid any harm. Spray-paint the spoons, then tie each one onto the rope to create an enchanting noisemaker that will liven up your backyard!

22. Painted Rocks as labels and decoration

These painted garden rocks are simple to make and will look great around your yard. You'll need some rocks that you can find in most yards, Mod Podge, acrylic paint, and rubber gloves (if you're using real glitter).

For this project, I like the idea of using rocks as labels for each plant container. Because let's face it; who remembers what's planted where? Let alone keeping up with watering! All jokes aside, these painted rocks would also make great borders or little stepping stones throughout your landscape beds. What do you think?

23. DIY Outdoor Chalkboard

A DIY Outdoor Chalkboard Wall is an easy way to expand the use of any outdoor space. You can use it as a menu or just jot down little notes to remember what needs doing when you're in the yard, like "turn on sprinklers" or "start weeding." It's especially helpful if there are multiple gardeners using the space because everyone will know what needs doing when!

24. Recycled Watering Can

Why buy a new watering can when you have so many things to recycle in the house?! You just need an empty milk jug or any other container that has a spout on its top, so you're set! Once it's done, just water whatever plants you're growing. This activity is super fun and educational too!

25. Mess-Free Bird Feeder

An old plastic bottle is all you need for this activity. Cut off its top, then poke some small holes on it before turning it into a bird feeder! Fill the bottom with birdseed, turn it upside down and place it outside to attract birds. This is one of those garden arts and crafts ideas that teach us about nature and how to respect and take care of animals.

26. Mailbox Garden Art

You can easily turn an old metal mailbox into a beautiful garden art to label where each plant comes from. All you need is some fabric or wrapping paper, then paint it with colorful scenes that show what's planted there, like sunflowers, for example. This will be super helpful if you are growing food in the backyard!

27. Garden Art with Pebbles

Turn your garden into an art gallery by creating a stunning piece of wall art that will decorate the entire outdoor space. All you need are some old jars, paint, and rocks! Simply fill them up with colorful pebbles before painting their lids to create beautiful jar garden art. After it dries out, just attach the lid back on each one of them to see your finished artwork.

28. Flower Bed Stencils

Make learning about flowers even more fun by turning flower beds into stencils! The best thing about this idea is that you can create as many stencil designs as there are types of plants in your garden! This way, every single plant bed will be unique. How to do it? Cut out flower shape stencils from thin cardboard, then simply place them where you want to draw next.

29. String Art

Making simple string art is one of those ingenious ideas that will teach you basic crafting skills while decorating the garden. All you need is wooden boards, nails, and some colorful thread. You can use nails to hammer the thread into place, then simply hang it up on a fence or wall! Don't forget to take help, so you don't hurt yourself.

30. DIY Wind Spinners

Spin your yard into a beautiful garden with these DIY Wind Spinners! You'll need some old CDs along with paper and fabric scraps. Simply cut out flowers and other shapes from different colors of paper before gluing them onto the discs, then paint as desired before hanging it up outside on some twine or rope

All the garden art and craft are pretty if done with love; just try to use available items rather than buying new stuff. Don't forget to take the assistance of adults when you are dealing with sharp and dangerous tools and materials. Now that we have our garden ready, it's time to enjoy it thoroughly!

Chapter 6: Enjoying your Garden

You may be worried about the fact that your garden is not perfect. It can be a little messy, or it may look too barren. Don't worry, just because it doesn't have flowers that you love right at this moment doesn't mean it won't have them soon!

All gardens go through distinct changes as different seasons pass by and knowing what to expect from each season will help you better enjoy your garden. You should also know how to maintain a clean and healthy garden so it can yield good results every time.

That's why harvesting is one of my favorite activities!

It's always fun picking vegetables like carrots that have been under the ground for months on end. Or maybe you're growing some tasty strawberries that would be great on top of ice cream!

No matter what it is, harvesting will be one of the best parts of gardening. As you pick your fruits and vegetables, you get to enjoy your fresh produce.

It's also time to plant trees so they

can start growing for next spring.

Some tips for enjoyable harvesting:

- Harvest early in the morning or late afternoon.
- If you're harvesting squash, wait until the fruit is fully mature and picked at its peak.
- Pick cucumbers when they're young and tender.
- Be careful with picking tomatoes because they are harder to grow than many other garden vegetables.
- Pick your fruit and vegetables early in the day, so if there is any bruising, it will be less noticeable on the surface of your produce.

- Harvesting makes you feel more connected with nature as well as the fact that every day spent in the garden yields new fruits and vegetables, which are fresh, healthy, tasty foods. So, enjoy the process.
- The best advice I can give you on harvesting is to be patient! If you plant something, wait until it's mature enough to pick. You'll know when it's ready because everything comes with its unique look or appearance.
- Also, with harvesting, you don't want to pick everything at once because if you leave some vegetables on the plant, they will continue to grow and provide more fresh produce later in the year when it's time for your garden to sleep during winter.
- Documenting the harvesting process will be a rewarding experience. It's important to always take notes on your progress because nothing is ever for certain!

- That's why it's good to keep a garden diary. It will help you remember which plants did well last year and how much effort you should put into them this time around. You don't ever want to forget about the small details because that one detail might be what makes or breaks your harvest.

In the end, what you'll get from all of this hard work is an abundant harvest that can feed your family and fill your pantry with fresh food. But you should also store your harvest properly.

How to store your harvest properly?

Different fruits and vegetables have different requirements.

Storing root veggies is quite simple; keep them in a cool, dry place where the temperature won't go over 50 degrees Fahrenheit.

Coolers are also great options for keeping your vegetables fresh. Just make sure they don't already have food inside them, so you don't contaminate your product with another plant's smell or taste!

Herbs like basil and sage can be stored by stem wrapping with tissue paper or in airtight containers with dampened (not wet) peat moss.

Tomatoes need to be kept away from cold air at all times because it will cause them to stop ripening which means no more juicy tomatoes for you unless you want to eat them green! Some people put tomatoes in a warm area and surround it with black plastic, but hanging them upside down is the best way to store them.

When harvesting vegetables like cucumbers, leafy greens, and herbs, it's good to harvest with scissors rather than tearing at the harvest with your hands or pulling at it.

If you're harvesting beans, don't forget to pick off the flowers so they'll keep growing more of those tasty treats we all love!

Finally, when selecting an area for storing fruits and vegetables, make sure that whatever place you choose keeps out pests like mice and insects like beetles and ants because they can ruin your harvest. Always check your produce for visible signs of infestation!

One of the most important things you can do when preserving your fruit and vegetables is to keep them out of the sun. If they sit under direct sunlight, they'll start to rot. It's also a good idea because the sun's rays contain some pollutants that will emit toxins into your produce if left in its light too long.

The last thing I want to tell you about harvesting is never waste anything! Even if it seems like nothing more than a tiny sprout or a branch that doesn't have much on it, every part of the plant has a purpose, whether for food or medicine.

The leaves might turn brown, but as long as there isn't any mold growing on them, just compost them and use them as fertilizer for next year's garden.

Every bit of plant has the potential to be food if you know what you're doing, so don't throw anything away!

Some ways of spending your best time in the garden and watching it grow!

One of the best ways to spend your time in the garden is by watching it grow! There are a lot of different things you can do if you have cultivated your garden.

- You can lay down in the grass and watch the clouds go by or pick flowers from your garden to make into bouquets.
- Another way to spend time is by taking care of bees so they can pollinate your plants or hunting for earthworms which will help with soil fertility.
- Make time for your friends and family – invite them over and grill burgers or steaks by the bonfire! They'll love spending time with you in your garden.
- Spend some time to plan out next year's layout. While also enjoying the weather while it lasts. Spending time and making memories with friends and family by hosting cookouts or grilling outside; also taking advantage of sunny days by relaxing outside, laying out with your outdoor furniture, playing games like ice skating, tobogganing, or sledding. Have gratitude towards nature for being able to enjoy outdoor space throughout the year.
- The break between seasons is a good opportunity to make sure everything is prepared for the next season.
- Make time to plant new annuals and perennials and order new seeds before the growing season starts.
- You can also dedicate time to pruning plants before the growing season starts.
- Sometimes it feels great to kill some time by making some compost for your garden; then, you'll be able to order new seeds or get them from the local plant store.
- It can also be fun to take advantage of windy days or where only brave hikers venture out by taking walks under the moonlight. Feel closer to nature while being one with it.
- As you get more experienced, you might consider getting a greenhouse so everything will keep growing even when it's snowing outside.
- Spend time journaling the current garden and creating a garden diary to look back on in the future.
- It's a good idea to take support and guidance from adults around you for creating your gardening community by joining or hosting a meetup with fellow gardeners; building a strong gardening community will raise support and encouragement for you throughout the seasons. You can also take your

- guardian's help in joining online forums or local gardening clubs to help each other out and share your knowledge about plants and animals that grow well in your region.
- Another thing you should consider is creating a scrapbook so family and friends can follow along on your progress.

There are plenty of other ways to spend quality time in your garden. However, the most important way to enjoy your time in the garden is harvesting anything that you might be growing at home!

Enjoying Springtime in Your Garden

Spring is one of those seasons where everything begins – new life, fresh blooms, and warmer weather!

Even though your garden may have lost its color during the winter, it will be ready to blossom again when spring arrives. The warmth of the sun helps tender plants break through the soil when you can finally see patches of greens emerging in your garden.

You can also expect to see many flowers in this season. Some of the most common signs that spring is arriving are when trees start sprouting leaves, early-bird chirping wakes you up in the morning, and when you see your garden turn bright green before your very eyes!

Knowing what to plant in your garden during this time would be a good idea so you can properly take care of them.

Enjoy this season by planting your flowers, veggies, and herbs. You may also want to add some new trees and shrubs that you feel would benefit your garden or yard.

Springtime is a great time to enjoy gardening and all the things that come with it – spending more time outdoors, enjoying nature, trying out gardening projects, etc.

Enjoy spring in your garden by doing different activities with friends and family, such as yoga, painting, and even making a bird feeder!

Water games are also a great way to spend your time in this season. Have fun by pouring water on each other!

Your garden will also receive more sunlight during spring, which means you should plant flowers that thrive in these conditions.

Have fun planting tulips, daffodils, roses, and snapdragons!

You can also begin pruning your fruit trees so they can bear better yields the following season. You may also want to start mowing your lawn or applying fertilizer on it if it needs some refreshing.

Enjoying springtime is all about enjoying the nature that surrounds you. Spend more time with your garden, and it will give back to you in many different ways!

Enjoying Summer in Your Garden

Once the spring season begins to settle out, you'll be able to see your garden come alive with all sorts of colors and blooms! So, enjoy the milder weather by planting flowers that are native to warm climates.

Enjoy this season by hosting activities like picnics or barbecues! Your garden is the perfect place to host these events because it can provide you with various settings, each one offering its unique charm.

For instance, you can set up an outdoor dining table that overlooks your garden or set out some lawn chairs near a koi pond under a willow tree.

In addition, you should know that the most important thing to consider during this season is watering. Even if it doesn't look like your garden needs water, make sure to check on it every day. You should test moisture levels using a finger – when you can easily press into the soil without resistance, then it's fine!

Finally, keep an eye out for bugs and insects in your garden because some plants attract them more than others. If you spot anything crawling around, simply get rid of them by spraying insecticides or other types of solutions over any affected areas.

Enjoying Fall in Your Garden

When fall rolls around again (which isn't very long since summer goes by quickly), there are several things you can do to make the most of this season.

First, rake up all the fallen leaves, so you don't have to deal with them later. They are great for your compost pile or mulch around your plants because they will help retain moisture in the soil. Plus, they'll keep weeds from popping up!

Next, it's time to prepare your garden for winter by laying down some wood chips or other protective materials across the base of each plant. Doing this will protect any tender new growth that may come up during springtime.
You should also wrap evergreen trees and shrubs tightly with burlap because their branches are used to staying warm year-round.

Enjoy this season by bringing in your outdoor furniture and lighting some candles or warming lanterns to set the mood. Arrange them around your fireplace or place where you can gather with friends and family! It's time to embrace everything about autumn – drink hot chocolate while strolling through the garden, toast marshmallows while enjoying dessert by the bonfire, or just simply relax under the sun.

Finally, don't hesitate to pick some flowers before they wilt because this is when they're at their best quality. As long as you cut them off right above a node on the stem, they can be enjoyed indoors.

Enjoying Winter in Your Garden

Winter is a reprieve from the busyness of the spring and summer months. During this time, you can work on planning next spring's garden layout or simply enjoy some quiet time in your outdoor sanctuary. Winter is a beautiful time to enjoy your outdoor space, but it can be quite challenging too! It's cold and wet, so all you really want to do is curl up next to the fire with a hot cup of tea or cocoa.

But before winter settles in for good, there are a few things that need to be done before you can officially start enjoying it. Usually, around November is the best time to plant trees because they don't require as much attention as other plants do. When planting evergreens, make sure to have them face south so they'll get plenty of sunlight during the peak growing season!

Finally, decorate your garden with all sorts of string lights so it looks festive year-round. You can also sled adorn poles with garlands made out of holly leaves, so everyone knows the holidays are coming! Also, you can break out the ice skates and grab a toboggan for those cold days when it seems just right to go tobogganing.

Enjoy this time of year by bringing out your holiday decorations and playing some festive music as you sip hot cocoa. Then just sit back and enjoy the serenity as snow drifts down from above!

The garden can be enjoyed at any season.

Spring brings new growth and life to plants after a dormant winter, it also brings weeding, pruning plants before the growing season starts, and getting to work in your garden. It allows you to enjoy the weather while it lasts.

Summer brings harvesting flowers, enjoying the garden with friends and family, grilling outside, or hosting cookouts, taking advantage of sunny days by relaxing outside, and laying out with your outdoor furniture.

While fall brings raking leaves into the compost pile or for use as mulch around your plants. Winter gives you time to plan for next spring's layout, enjoying quiet time in your outdoor sanctuary, planting trees, decorating, and playing festive music as you sip hot cocoa or play games like ice skating, tobogganing, and sledding.

With this, our beautiful journey reaches a conclusion! I am sure you enjoyed reading it as much as I enjoyed writing it.

Leave a 1-click review!

I would be incredibly grateful if you take just 60 seconds to write just a brief review on Amazon, even if it's just a few sentences.

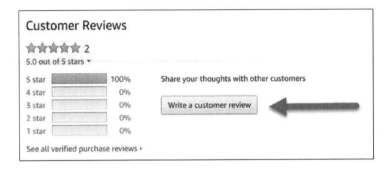

https://www.amazon.com/review/create-review-asin=B09ML95Q6N

Conclusion

Gardening is not just for growing food; it is also a science that helps improve lives by reconnecting people with nature. Whether you have a green thumb or are just starting out, gardening is a rewarding and time-honored tradition that everyone should experience in their childhood.

A child who actively enjoys gardening will have a better connection with the food they eat and will be more prepared to take care of their very own garden as adults.

They will also find that organic gardening is a lot of fun and could easily become a hobby or even a career option as they grow older.

It's an opportunity for you to develop your green thumb, and it's also a chance to grow healthier produce for your family and friends.

This e-book has shown you how to gain the necessary knowledge and skills to start your own garden and be successful every step of the way. It's going to be your companion rather than a one-time read.

There's no need to spend all day in front of the e-book; you can learn and try the methods simultaneously, then learn more and implement them further. You can learn at your pace in your own time in the comfort of your home.

Utilize the knowledge given in this e-book to have the best garden ever, not just for yourself but also for your family and community.

Remember, practice makes perfect, so keep taking notes and keep iterating until you get it right. Whatever happens, never give up because even mistakes can turn into great rewards with enough effort. There is much more to gardening for kids than just producing food; it's also about caring for our natural resources.

It takes patience and practice, so don't get frustrated if your plants don't grow the way you want them to. Keep learning more about how they work so you can become a true gardening genius!

A failure is only a failure if it isn't followed by success; always keep that in mind when something doesn't go your way because there's always room for improvement! Even if what you did was an honest mistake, learn from it and keep going because you'll never know if something will work unless you try it out.

Soon you will realize that gardening is a hobby for life!

It teaches you to take care of your surroundings while also teaching you patience, perseverance, responsibility, and more. It encourages healthy eating habits by teaching you where food comes from and how easy it is to grow your own food.

Gardening requires some upfront work (choosing which seeds or plants one would like to grow) with long-term benefits (harvesting your crop). Be prepared to spend some time outside in order to reap the benefits.

You will be the sole caretaker of your garden. So, be sure that you are ready and willing to take responsibility. But don't let that intimidate or overwhelm you but also be prepared to learn as much as possible before getting started.

It will take some experience and knowledge in order for it to become successful; however, with learning and patience, it can be well worth it!

You are responsible for your own success, so make sure to always read up on how things work before implementing them into practice. Believe me, taking notes is very beneficial because every time you do something differently, write down what happened so you can better understand what's going on.

The most important takeaway from this e-book is that in gardening, you'll always discover something new to learn and try, making it an endlessly fascinating experience.

It is also comforting to know that even if you aren't the most natural-born green thumb, there's always room for improvement as long as you keep learning more about plants.

Never give up on your garden because mistakes can turn into great rewards with enough effort and patience. Above all, don't forget to appreciate what we have and conserve whatever we can because nature is precious.

This ebook is my special gift to you. I have added my experience and tricks from my personal gardening journal. You can use it to inspire yourself, family members, and friends through education and action. Sow the seeds of knowledge so those good things may grow within your community, nation, and beyond!

It will help you in uncovering the secrets of successful gardening.

My advice to you is to enjoy what you are learning and know that anything is possible with determination, practice, and the right information. Gardening is not a task but rather a way of life. It's about caring for our earth, our environment, and most importantly, it teaches you to take responsibility for what you are doing!

I'm glad we undertook this journey together because now you're ready to begin your own garden with the proper tools for success! Whether it's for food or just to add beauty to one's life, Gardening is a rewarding experience. If you enjoy nature, this ebook will be a great starting point in your gardening journey.

You must also ensure that you work with nature, not against it. Refrain from activities which damage or pollute the environment. Practice sustainable gardening practices that help the biodiversity and production of healthy food.

Most importantly, keep trying and never give up because every day is a chance to start fresh! Now you can refer back to this e-book while planning your next gardening session and make sure it's an enjoyable and fruitful one.

Don't forget to enjoy yourself as you cultivate beauty, health, and prosperity!

Now go out there and get your hands dirty!

But before you go, please share a review on Amazon so that other children can also discover the secret to your gardening success.

My other books you will love!

Amazon.com/dp/B09MLBKYFS

Amazon.com/dp/B09ML9VJCF

Don't forget to grab your GIFT!!!

http://daphnemcooper.com/parenting.pdf

Joining the PME Community

Looking to meet other parents that can help you on your parenting journey? If so, then check out the Parenting Made Easy (PME) Community here:

https://www.facebook.com/groups/293830159257919/

References

- Types of Plants

Types of Plants: Annual, Perennial and Biennial | Teleflora Blog

- Growing plants with stem cutting.

Plant Propagation by Stem Cutting | Types of Stem Cuttings (ugaoo.com)

- Tools for Gardening

Gardening for kids : Tools to get them started - Kids n Clicks

- Theme Gardening.

Gardening With Kids Using Themes - Gardening Know How

Kids Gardening: Tips, Ideas and Projects | Planet Natural

Down to Earth : Garden Secrets! Garden Stories! Garden Projects You Can Do! By Michael J. Rosen. Harcourt Brace, ISBN: 0152013415.

- Garden Art

kidzkorner - ICanGarden.com

Garden Crafts for Kids: 50 Great Reasons to Get Your Hands Dirty. By Diane Rhoades. ISBN: 0806909994.

Learn to Grow! The Fun of Gardening For Children (gardenforever.com)

Made in the USA
Monee, IL
30 April 2022